Exploring Rock Pools

Written by Jill McDougall

Contents

Rock Pools

Look!
The **tide** is out.
It has left pools
of water between
the rocks!

rock pools

There are lots of interesting animals
in rock pools.
Let's see what we can find...

3

Starfish

Starfish can be found in rock pools.
They have five spiny arms.
Their eyes are on the ends of their arms.

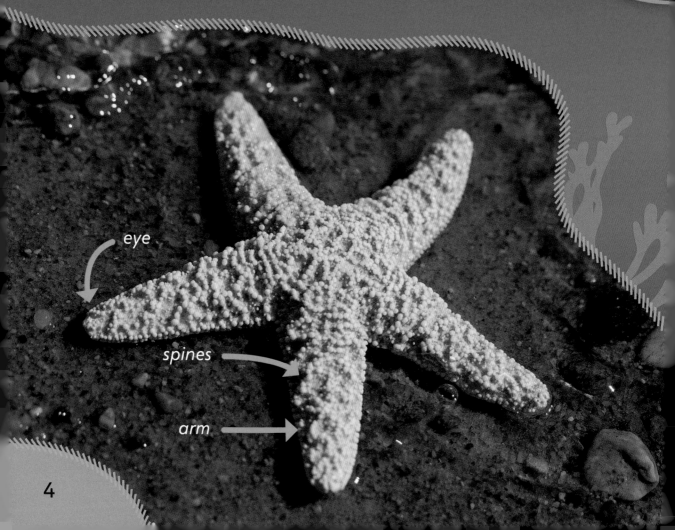

eye

spines

arm

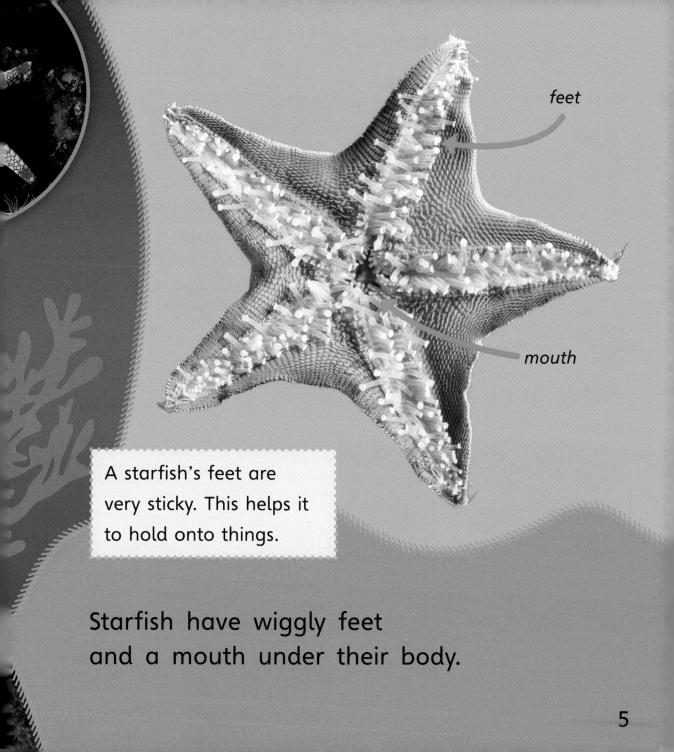

feet

mouth

A starfish's feet are
very sticky. This helps it
to hold onto things.

Starfish have wiggly feet
and a mouth under their body.

Crabs

Crabs can be found in rock pools.
They hide under rocks or in the sand.

Some crabs cover
their shells with **seaweed**
to help them hide.

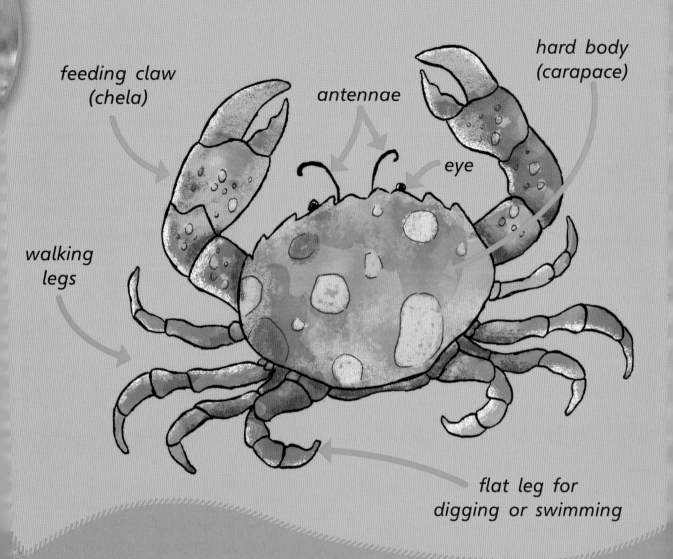

feeding claw
(chela)

antennae

hard body
(carapace)

eye

walking
legs

flat leg for
digging or swimming

Crabs are not fussy eaters.
They munch on old seaweed
and dead fish.

Limpets

Limpets are a kind of sea snail. They have a shell like a pointy hat that protects their soft body.

shell

head

soft body

Limpets eat algae. They use their
shell to scrape it from rocks.

Limpets make a hole in a rock.
This hole is their home.
They climb out of their home
to feed on **algae**.

Fish

Small fish can be found in rock pools. They dart into little cracks in the rocks to hide from danger.

Fish have eyes near the top of their head. This helps them to look out for danger.

Some fish can crawl on their **fins**.
These fish are called blennies.
They crawl to a new rock pool when
they need to find food.

What Can You See?

Look closely!
Which animals can you see?

Rock Pool Quiz

Which animals are these?

1 I have a shell like a pointy hat.

2 I have fins.

3 I have a mouth but no head.

4 I eat dead fish.

Find the answers to this quiz on page 16.

Glossary

algae   simple plants with no roots or leaves

fins   parts of a fish that help it to swim

seaweed   plants that grow in saltwater

tide   flow of the seas to and from the land

Answers   **1** limpet   **2** fish   **3** starfish   **4** crab